CW00431360

DEFENDING THE COAST

World War Two Defences at Clacton-on-Sea Holland-on-Sea & Jaywick

by

Clacton VCH Group

Elizabeth Austin
Hazel Beckham
Roger Kennell
Colin H Preen
Bob Rawson
Cindy Rowland
Tim Underwood

Cover illustration: Anti-invasion defences at West Clacton
Photograph courtesy of Imperial War Museum, London

DEFENDING THE COAST
World War Two Defences at
Clacton-on-Sea
Holland-on-Sea & Jaywick

Clacton VCH Group

Every attempt has been made to trace copyright. The authors apologise if any images have been reproduced inadvertently without copyright.

ISBN 978-0-9546458-1-6

Published by Clacton VCH group

V C H Essex
Essex Record Office
Chelmsford
Essex
CM2 6YT
www.essexpast.net

Printed by Keith Avis Printers
68 High Street Hadleigh Suffolk
01473 823366

Contents

DEFENDING THE COAST

Preface

This booklet is the culmination of some three years work by a small group of volunteers, guided by a military archaeologist, who are passionate about the history of Clacton, Holland on Sea and Jaywick.

The Clacton VCH Group was formed in 2002, under the tutelage of the Essex Victoria County History, to research aspects of the modern history of the area. Their first project was a comprehensive investigation of the Second World War period. During this work, the opportunity arose to apply for a grant from the Heritage Lottery Fund to survey and record the Second World War defences of the Clacton area. The application was successful and the group was fortunate to have their work directed by Mr Fred Nash of the Historic Environment Branch, Essex County Council. The full report of the project was published in May 2008 and copies of this weighty tome can be consulted in the local library.

This booklet is a digest of that report, designed to give the reader a flavour of the enormous effort that turned a popular seaside resort into a fortress ready to resist an invasion. When walking through Clacton today, nearly 70 years after the fortification of the area, there is little to be seen of the gun emplacements, tank traps, minefields and other defences that were constructed in a matter of months in 1940. It must be remembered that these were desperate times. The defeat of the British Expeditionary Force in France and their miraculous evacuation at Dunkirk was expected to be followed by a full-scale invasion. In the summer of 1940, it was not known whether this would come on the South Coast or the East Coast and Clacton could have found itself in the front line of a battle to save the country. With this in mind, an extraordinary effort was made to protect the area against a possible imminent attack.

The booklet explains the extent of the defensive works, and their eventual removal, and tells you where to look for the few remains of fortress Clacton.

Acknowledgements

The members of the Clacton VCH Group are most grateful to the Essex Record Office, and the Clacton Public Library where much of the research work was carried out to identify the defence works, and the details of their subsequent removal, which has enabled this booklet to come to fruition. Further help came from the Clacton & District Local History Society and the resource of the late Kenneth Walker.

The fieldwork was carried out by the Clacton VCH Group with Fred Nash, Military Archaeologist for Essex County Council. The project, to research and report on the anti-invasion defences of Clacton and district, provided the group with an understanding of defence types and their remains.

The work could not have been successfully completed without the considerable help of local people and the co-operation of the landowners. Thanks are also extended to Ann and Colin Preen for their hospitality, allowing their home to be used as a base for the major part of the project.

The group acknowledges the assistance of Fred Nash, and Dr. Chris Thornton of VCH Essex, for their involvement in assuring the accuracy of this publication.

1

Clacton-on-Sea prior to the invasion scare

A thriving seaside resort

The West Parade and Gardens at Clacton-on-Sea during the 1930's

Founded in 1871, Clacton-on-Sea rapidly developed after the construction of the pier in that same year. The pier's purpose was to land the summer time day trippers, who arrived by paddle steamers from Tower Pier, London. Building development soon began with roads laid out and all the infrastructure necessary to support the birth of the new town.

Progress was rapid and sustained to construct a community whose purpose was to provide a welcome for visitors and holidaymakers. Those visitors came in ever increasing numbers. The railway came in 1882, the pier was lengthened and improved in stages, and the Clacton Urban District Council (CUDC) came into being in 1894. Private enterprise brought the Palace pleasure complex to the seafront, also Riggs Retreat for entertainment, and a Bandstand. New churches and their parishes were created, private education and convalescence establishments opened. And there were the boarding houses, guest houses and hotels to provide accommodation for the ever increasing numbers of visitors and holidaymakers.

The decade of the 1930's revealed a town that had progressed into one of the country's leading summer resorts, offering a wide range of attractions, from theatres, gardens, cinemas, shops and amusements, and of course the golden sands and safe swimming. Confidence among the local authority officers and businessmen concerned with the holiday business, and indeed within the town itself, was high with the approach of each new summer season. The town's growth and success seemed unstoppable.

Visitors came to Clacton-on-Sea to enjoy themselves, and forget the situation in Nazi Germany which was steadily developing during the 1930's. It was the 'Munich Crisis' of 1938 which brought the visible sign of the increased tension to the town, for on the west greensward A.R.P. (Air Raid Precautions) trenches were being dug.

The Clacton Urban District Council had Air Raid Precautions on the agenda at all their council meetings since 1937. Preparatory work and research by the CUDC in response to central government and Essex County Council directives gathered apace, but many residents, and certainly the holidaymakers, were largely unaware of all these preparations.

September 1939, and war is declared

The 1939 summer holiday season was starting to draw towards its final few weeks, before the long winter months began. The council officials were already making preparations for the following 1940 season, and compiling the new official holiday guide.

Despite the apparent concentration on the holiday business within the town, there had been preparations for war through the A.R.P. directives which had been received by the CUDC. These had come via the Essex County Council and Central Government, to implement provisions to protect the populace from enemy air attacks, which was the new fear in warfare. A separate A.R.P. committee was formed who reported to the full

Council. Reports prepared for the CUDC indicate the scope of preparations from the provision of a range of equipment from gas masks, stirrup pumps and buckets, to air raid shelters.

The declaration of war on the 3rd September 1939 gave added impetus to the protection of the populace, and A.R.P. provision and the training of personnel continued. The period of the so called 'Phoney War' then began with little appearing to happen. However into the early months of 1940, and the reality of war was brought to the town, early in February, with a huge explosion rocking the town. A drifting German mine, had hit the pier close to the lifeboat house ripping a gaping hole in the wooden decking.

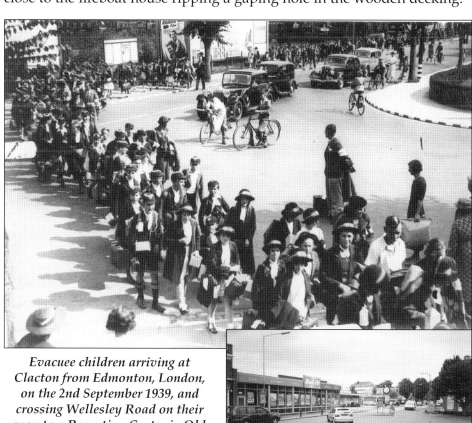

Evacuee children arriving at Clacton from Edmonton, London, on the 2nd September 1939, and crossing Wellesley Road on their way to a Reception Centre in Old Road. A comparative view from 2009 is also included.

Photograph courtesy of the Imperial War Museum, London. Hu 5476; and Fred Nash, ECC

The next incident in the town was to have an effect nationally. On the evening of the 30th April, just before midnight, a damaged German Heinkel 111 mine-laying plane crashed in Victoria Road. The crew of four died, but the crash, and subsequent exploding of a mine, also killed Mr and Mrs Gill the first people to lose their lives on mainland Britain as a result of enemy action. Clacton suddenly made unwelcome headlines. Those involved in the Clacton-on-Sea holiday business were furious that the adverse publicity would have a serious effect on the forthcoming season. Sadly, for the first time since the founding of Clacton-on-Sea, there was to be no 1940 summer season. On 10th May the Germans invaded the Low Countries, and the war situation moved quickly, the Nazis sweeping across Belgium and France. The British Expeditionary Force (BEF) were pushed in retreat to the beaches of Dunkirk. The invasion of this country was now a real and immediate threat.

On the last day of April 1940, a German mine-laying plane crashed on Victoria Road. One of the mines it was carrying exploded, and completely demolished a house which once stood in the foreground of this picture

2

The WWII defences of Clacton-on-Sea, Holland-on-Sea and Jaywick

Invasion Expected

The Secretary for War, Anthony Eden, broadcast to the nation on the 14th May 1940, with a National appeal on the wireless for the creation of a Local Defence Volunteer (LDV) force, later re-named the Home Guard. Within two days nearly 500 local men had reported to the Clacton Police Station between the ages of 17 to 65.

Events now began to move rapidly. On the 21st May 1940, a Military Restricted Area was imposed on the town, which impinged upon the residents' freedom of movement. The restricted area referred to the beach and the promenade; and at points along the greensward to which access was denied through Military Operations. These restrictions increased the following month when the Eastern Regional Commissioner placed Clacton-on-Sea, and other local resorts, under a ban to holidaymakers. The restrictions stated that:

"No person may stay for a holiday, recreation, pleasure or as a casual wayfarer."

The Royal Engineers were then tasked to breach the pier to prevent its use by the enemy. Marine Parade was closed in preparation for when the explosive charges were activated. This proved a wise decision for in addition to the pier being breached, many panes of glass were shattered at seafront properties, including the Band Pavilion, tea shops and the former Beaumont Hall Hotel. The Crystal Casino and the Childrens Theatre on the pier were then soon to be demolished. The Military further wished to dismantle the Steel Stella ride, but the pier owner, Ernest Kingsman, engaged his solicitors to prevent this from happening. He was successful. The Royal Engineers work was carried out from the 25th May and concluded on the 1st July.

The Clerk to the Clacton Urban District Council received a secret and urgent letter on the 30th May from the Ministry of Transport (M.O.T.), Roads Department, regarding Emergency Measures, stating that:

"all direction signs on public highways in rural and built up areas in your district should be removed and stored."

A tangle of defence wiring on the cliffs opposite Lyndhurst Road in 1943.
Photograph courtesy of TDC

The signs necessary for removal were only those where the actual place name appeared. Such was the urgency of the situation, the M.O.T. demanded that the clerk reply the following day with a report by telephone of progress on the removal work!

The town had two pleasure piers. The main pier was at Pier Gap; but a second and shorter pier, more correctly called The Jetty, stood opposite

Pillboxes were built all along the local coastline. This pillbox was built into the pre-war sea wall at Holland-on-Sea opposite Southview Drive.
Photograph courtesy of TDC

Wash Lane. Where there were cliffs opposite the main pier, towards Wash Lane these diminished in height, making a vulnerable landing area for the enemy. The Jetty was therefore totally demolished, with the work commencing on 6th June 1940.

The desperate evacuation of the British Expeditionary Force from Dunkirk (the Clacton lifeboat was among the many 'Little Ships' which helped in the evacuation) heightened the necessity for increasing anti-invasion defences. The L.D.V. was manning temporary road blocks from June. Enemy aircraft activity over the town was now increasing, and searchlights and guns were brought into position along the clifftop. Trees were cut down and some shelters were removed along the seafront to allow unrestricted views, and uninterrupted fields of fire.

Clacton-on-Sea, a well defended town

From the Spring of 1940 the construction of a co-ordinated system of defence works was undertaken along the whole of the Tendring coastline. The impetus for these works was partly driven by a recent British Military report which had identified the twelve coastal towns in the British Isles most vulnerable to an enemy attack. Clacton-on-Sea and neighbouring Frinton-on-Sea both appeared on this list.

A Description of the Defence Types

Defence types were many and various, depending on the vulnerability of the position to be defended. Broadly, the obstacles and weapon emplacements could be broken down into three main types; those sited to defend against a seaborne landing on the beaches, those to prevent the armoured divisions running riot if they gained a foothold in the towns and

Every road leading off the seafront was sealed by a road barrier. This rare photograph shows the anti-tank pimples and barbed wire at the junction of Colne Road with Marine Parade East, Clacton-on-Sea.
Photograph courtesy of Clacton & District Local History Society

fields immediately inland, and those to counter the strong possibility of an airborne attack by paratroopers.

A short description of some of them:

The **Alan-Williams** turret was a steel rotating dome set into the ground as a strong point. It was manned by two infantrymen with a mounted machine gun.

Concrete blocks for anti-tank use were approximately 1m square cubes arranged to block tanks and other vehicles.

Concrete pimples for anti-tank use were cone-shaped, but truncated in height. Laid in wide belts, they are often called "dragons teeth."

Dannert and Apron wiring, commonly known as barbed wire.

Minefields were areas where anti-personnel explosives had been sown.

Pillboxes were concrete strong points for a section of infantrymen.

This wartime picture shows the anti-invasion scaffolding on the beach at The Gap, Holland-on-Sea, which sealed off access to the cliff top.
Photograph courtesy of TDC

Poles were long wooden poles set upright over a wide area in open ground, to discourage airborne landings.

Road blocks used a range of means to provide a barrier at important locations.

Rails were removable lengths of rail track, set upright in sockets at a road block.

Metal tubular **scaffolding** erected as a long fence on vulnerable beaches, provided an anti-invasion obstacle to landing craft and tanks.

Slit trenches were a common means of providing infantrymen with a defence position.

A **spigot mortar** was a cheap, easily manufactured gun, issued to the Home Guard and usually mounted onto a cylindrical concrete base.

A **weapon pit** was an excavated defence point, often protected by sandbagging.

A description and location of the anti-invasion defences at Clacton-on-Sea.

Much of the Clacton seafront is cliffs. The main anti-invasion defences were sited on the beach, at the cliff face, and on the cliff top, with others at strategic points around the rear of the town to prevent it being taken by a surprise attack from inland, perhaps by paratroopers.

Fortunately in recent investigations a wealth of contemporary data has been found to still survive. This includes a detailed record of all the defence positions built on private land with the seafront hotels featuring prominently, RAF aerial photographs from the 1940's which are so clear that individual anti-tank pimples can be counted, and a military plan of the seafront showing the anti-invasion scaffolding, pillboxes, Alan-Williams turrets, barbed wire and road barriers. Clacton Urban District Council kept plans of the many minefields around the town, and correspondence relating to their eventual clearance. This valuable archive has now surfaced, to provide us with an insight into the problems experienced, after the war in once more making these lethal areas safe.

West of Clacton Pier

As the primary anti-invasion obstacle on the beach, there was a continuous length of scaffolding on the beach approximately between High and Low Water Marks, from the pier westwards. This scaffolding was approximately ten feet high and consisted of two rows of vertical tubes, connected with four rows of horizontal tubes, braced with twin rows of raking tubes. This barrier certainly extended to Wash Lane and probably continued all the way past the former Butlins Holiday Camp, which was then being used as a base for the Pioneer Corps and a anti-aircraft gunnery training school, to Jaywick and beyond.

At the back of the beach there were barbed wire entanglements on steel stakes and behind this, stretching the length of the promenade from Collingwood Road to Clacton Golf Course, was a long row of huge concrete blocks, hundreds of them, each one a chest-high cube weighing several tons. To present an impenetrable barrier to both tanks and infantry the blocks were cast no more than three feet apart, staggered, and covered with more barbed wire.

On the lower promenade, close to Trafalgar Road there was a pillbox, with another 300 yards away opposite Penfold Road. On the cliff-top path were two further pillboxes just off centre to those on the promenade.

The Pier Gap

The pier gap was well defended. The gap provided a potential access point for the invader. Concrete blocks were positioned on the two ramped areas either side of the pier approach from the beach. In pier gap itself there were three weapon pits, the whole area being surrounded by wiring. Additionally, just into Pier Avenue, there was a concrete road barrier.

East of Clacton Pier

There were three weapon positions on top of the Band Pavilion complex, and at least a further eleven, some of which may have been Alan-Williams turrets, along the cliff up to First Avenue. On the lower promenade below Orwell Road there was a pillbox. More pillboxes were sited below

The beach and cliffs at Eastcliff. Rows of defence wiring line the shore,
the structure on the cliff top conceals a pillbox, while on the greensward
is a minefield.
Photograph courtesy of TDC

Anglefield, at Thoroughgood and Russell Roads, and below Lancaster and
Connaught Gardens.With the absence of anti-invasion scaffolding east of
the pier, or a dense run of anti-invasion blocks, the defence planners were
clearly concerned about the possibility of German tanks being able to land
and climb the cliffs. Wherever this seemed likely, up the cliff paths or where
the slope was more shallow, short runs of concrete blocks were cast. This
was clearly easier to do on the path itself or at its edge. Between the pier
and First Avenue there were no fewer than ten of these anti-tank barriers,
the longest some 70 cubes in length.

Like the West side of the pier, the East side also had pillboxes along the
clifftop. They were at Anglefield, St. Pauls Road and at Connaught
Gardens. Unlike the West side of the pier, on the lower promenade only at
Anglefield did the pillbox coincide with one on the lower promenade.

At Eastcliff, at the further end of the Marine Parade East, The Lilley Farm Beach was covered with wiring at the foot of the cliffs, and also had a defence post.

Road barriers

The seafront defences previously described offered a substantial defence barrier, but there was an even more daunting barrier for any invader, which extended from St. Vincent Road at West Clacton to Connaught Gardens East at the far end of the seafront. This continuous barrier was composed of the properties themselves along the Marine Parades, West and East. The properties included private residences, hotels and guest houses and the St. Michaels Convent. These buildings provided a physical barrier, between which in their gardens, on the pavements and on the actual road junctions, there were multiple rows of concrete pimples and wiring. Removable rails were provided across St. Vincent Road, and Anglefield, Vista Road and Connaught Gardens West. This immense barrier, at its western end, extended into the junction of Freeland Road and Wash Lane.

At Beach Road, where the junction with the Marine Parade East is shaped as a bell-mouth, there was a need for extra defence. Here at number 19 Marine Parade East, the military converted the front room, the landing and kitchen into a fortified position with its associated wiring. At nearby Anglefield, the ornamental gardens and shrubs were all removed by the military to make a clear field of fire.

The combined anti-invasion defences on the beach, promenade, cliffs and along the Marine Parade provided a formidable system. To construct these defences local builders were employed. H J Smith and C H Chaston were two of those who carried out the work. Later, larger national contractors were used. The Regular Army were responsible for overseeing the work erecting the beach scaffolding. The scope of the defence types which were constructed, and the urgency with which they were completed, was a major achievement.

Road blocks

The main built up area inland had controlled entrance and exit road blocks across at least nine of the roads into the town. These road blocks were located as follows:

A defence point on London Road looking towards the present St. John's Road roundabout. In March 1941 a party of war correspondents toured Eastern Command to observe the troops training. The sandbagged defence post alongside the barrier was manned by men of the 6th Northamptonshire Regiment. In 2007 the scene hardly appears to have changed.
Photograph courtesy of the Imperial War Museum, London. H7943 and Fred Nash, ECC

West Road; just beyond the entrance to the Clacton Golf Clubhouse.
Cloes Lane; at the junction with Douglas Road.
London Road; close to the allotments.
St. Johns Road; at the junction of North Road.
St. Johns Road; between the junctions of North Road and Old Road.
Valley Road; at its junction with Holland Road.
Sladburys Lane; at the junction with Holland Road.
Holland Road; between the junctions of Sladburys Lane and Hillside Crescent.

At least four of these road blocks, Cloes Lane, London Road, West Road, and Sladburys Lane, had an attendant concrete pillbox.

Minefields

Minefields were laid in addition to, or in place of other defences. Starting from Holland Marshes, between Holland Brook and what is now the car park, there was an irregular shaped minefield. West of York Road the minefield extended along the cliff top and down the cliff face almost to Kings Avenue. A rectangular section of the cliff top between Kings Avenue to Hazlemere Road was mined[1]. From Sea Lane to First Avenue on the broad greensward there was a 400 yard long minefield, which contained 216 mines laid in four rows parallel to the sea. A barbed wire fence surrounded this and the other minefields. The next batch of minefields was a considerable distance away on the Clacton Golf Course. Here were four irregular shaped minefields. Two soldiers of the 221 Infantry Brigade of the Essex Beach Division were tragically killed when creating these minefields. Beyond Golf Green Road was a further minefield at Jaywick, which although recorded and given a site identification number, was later concluded to be a dummy field.

Contemporary photographic evidence at the West Greensward, Clacton, shows barbed wire and a wooden sign on a stake, stating 'Danger Minefield'[2]. This was probably a dummy minefield. There was no military record attributed to this site and the consecutive military reference numbering system from Holland Haven places the next minefields at the Clacton Golf Course.

---

1 During the mine clearance works from 1945, no actual mines were found here. It was therefore believed that this was a dummy minefield.
2 G. Elcoat, Anti-Invasion Preparations on the Essex Coast. 1940-41 (1960): copy in ERO reference library.

Another type of mine was the Canadian Pipe Mine. They were positioned under roads but had a restricted use in the town, only two sites being known. Two of these mines were at Great Clacton, ten yards east of the Queens Head. The other location was at Burcarts Corner, Old Road, where there were three under Old Road and another just into Wellesley Road. There were no other anti-invasion defences at this point, unlike the pipe mines near the Queens Head which were placed to support the road blocks.

Schedule of Minefields

Military Number	Location
45/40	Holland Marshes, near Holland Brook
45/41 & 41a	Holland-on-Sea cliffs between York Road and Hazlemere Rd
45/42	The Greensward from Sea Lane to First Avenue
45/43, 44, 45 & 46	Clacton Golf Course
45/47	Jaywick between Golf Green Road and Meadow Way, (dummy)

Minefields were a part of the anti-invasion defences.
This minefield sign on the West Greensward related to a dummy minefield,
no mines were ever laid in this location.
Photograph courtesy of Clacton and District Local History Society

Poles

A seaborne invasion was not the only method the enemy might attempt. An airborne assualt, or a combination of the two, had to be defended against. Tall wooden poles, with wiring, were set up in open fields in the northern area of Great Clacton to frustrate a landing. Coppins Hall Farm fields, and Kiln Barn Farm and nearby Brook Farm, both in the vicinity of the present Brookvale complex, had fields containing these poles. Around the Cooks Green area, Cooks Green Farm, Lodge Farm and Dairy House Farm all had poles and wiring erected in some of their fields. At Little Clacton, more farms had poles erected across them.

A miscellany

Clacton pier, already breached by a floating German mine which hit the pier and exploded in February 1940, was further breached by the Royal Engineers using explosives to make a 75 feet gap. This was to prevent its use for any attempted landing. These demolition works took place from 25th May 1940.

Throughout the town there were numerous defended points in the form of weapon pits or trenches. On land opposite the former Sodbury House in Valley Road, close to the Oxford Road junction, there were four gun pits along a boundary, with a concrete shelter in a small copse and wiring on two sides. Further along this road at Valley Farm, there were extensive works, including eight large gun pits, and weapon pits, all with associated trenches and wiring. In Cotswold Road on the Bull Hill Estate, there were forty rifle pits. St. John's Vicarage did not escape the defence works, as here was excavated a large defence post and trench. Everyday necessities had to be catered for. At Jubilee Avenue, still at Great Clacton, timber buildings were erected for use as a kitchen. Nearby were some field lavatories, and here were further trenches, as protection for those using the lavatories!

At the Holland Park area, there were various defence posts, including two field gun positions, all with their associated wiring. At the old London Road at Brookers Farm, currently the Robin Hood public house, there was a weapon trench, and a weapon pit. On the St. John's Road at Pathfields, sandbags were used to form defence works.

Further defence works were centred around Southcliff Park, Rush Green and Alton Park Farm as well as more individual locations. To maximise the effectiveness of many of these defence posts, wooden fences were removed or reduced in height, and in one case advertising hoardings were taken down. At Anglefield, shrubs were cut down on the triangular garden dividing Carnarvon Road. At 'The Gardens' on Marine Parade East, further shrubs were removed and turf taken up.

Meticulous records were kept. For example, a beach hut named 'Skylarks' was requisitioned and moved to Gainsboro' Avenue for use as a store hut by the military!

The Construction programme
It was the evacuation of the British Expeditionary Force (B.E.F.) from the beaches of Dunkirk, during May/June 1940, which prompted a real fear of imminent invasion of this country. It was popularly supposed that any invasion would be on the South East coasts of Kent and Sussex, but a British Military report had identified that the Frinton to Clacton coastline was also vulnerable to invasion. From records made during the war, some minefields were laid as early as March 1940, while construction works began in June with pillboxes, and the main roadblocks. Property and land was also requisitioned. Later in the year work was underway on the concrete pimples and wiring at the road junctions on the seafront. This work continued into 1941, when further pillboxes were constructed. These main defences were then supported by a wide range of subsidiary weapon pits, trenches and wiring built mostly from 1942 and extending even into 1943. Thus the creation of the anti-invasion defences at Clacton were an on- going process in spite of the threat of invasion diminishing from 1942.

Associated defences: Searchlights, Heavy Anti-Aircraft gun sites and 'Diver' gun sites. In addition to the defences installed against the threat of a full seaborne invasion, there was also defences against an airborne attack. These consisted of searchlights, anti-aircraft guns and 'diver' gun sites.

A searchlight unit is recorded as being on the greensward at Marine Parade East, opposite Connaught Gardens West. Another searchlight was located just to the West of the old Martello Tower on the edge of Clacton Golf Club course. Inland of the main built-up area of the town were two further

A gunsite located on the West Greensward. Codenamed Diver, they were set up in 1944 to combat the VI flying bombs. The comparative view shows that the site is easily identifiable today.
Photograph courtesy of Derek Johnson, and Fred Nash, ECC

searchlights, one at Willow Farm which was south of Cooks Green, and the other at Duchess Farm off St. Johns Road but actually within St. Osyth parish. Pathfields Road was the location of another searchlight site.

Heavy Anti-Aircraft (H.A.A.) gun sites were located at Holland Haven, designated as C4, and believed to have been constructed some-time between July 1941 and May 1942, and another at Jaywick, designated as C3. This site was at Park Square, before the present building development work had began. Eventually this site was provided with concrete emplacements for four 3.7" guns, which were all grouped together, with some Nissen huts.

The 'Diver' gun sites, composed of similar guns, had a different lay-out and purpose. A new type of weapon, the V1 popularly known either as the 'Doodlebug', 'Buzz-bomb', 'Flying-bomb', or the 'Fly-bomb', was being targeted at this country. During late 1944 three local sites were established to meet this new menace.

Site 1. On Clacton Golf Course, towards the seaward side of the course, approached by a new concrete road.

A view from the observation tower of the six-inch coastal artillery gun site opposite Hazlemere Road looking towards Clacton-on-Sea, showing extensive camouflage netting covering the battery. Just visible at the top right is the Cliff Cafe next to Sea Lane.

Photograph courtesy of the Imperial War Museum, London. H 15765.

Another view of the same site. Beyond is the concrete observation tower for the battery.
Photograph courtesy of the Imperial War Museum, London. H 15763.

This view was clearly taken from close to the cliff edge.
Photograph courtesy of the Imperial War Museum, London. H 15764.

Site 2. At the end of the West Greensward, just off the promenade, opposite the present Bowling Green.

Site 3. Off the B1032 road at the bottom of the Little Holland Hall hill towards Great Holland.

'Diver' gun sites were distinguished by the guns being positioned in a linear alignment. It is recorded that these gunners had an impressive record of 'hits' against the in-coming V1's.

A description and location of the anti-invasion defences at Holland-on-Sea

In 1939 Holland-on-Sea was still developing from the ancient village of Little Holland. There were no sea defences, and many roads were still unmade, including the sea-front road named the Kings Parade. There were still a large number of overgrown undeveloped building plots. The anti-invasion defences at Holland-on-Sea were of a different character to those at Clacton-on-Sea, as demanded by its physical location and its partially undeveloped situation.

This pre-war pavilion in 1942 opposite York Road at Holland-on-Sea, provided the perfect camouflage for a concrete pillbox
Photograph courtesy of TDC

Defences on the beach, showing three different anti-invasion defence types: anti-tank blocks, wiring and scaffolding.
Photograph courtesy of the Imperial War Museum, London. H 11554.

A view from the Martello Tower 'E' near the present Hastings Avenue,
Clacton-on-Sea, showing the depth of the anti-invasion defences
with scaffolding, anti-tank blocks and defence wiring.
Photograph courtesy of the Imperial War Museum, London. H 11554.

Soldiers checking the defence scaffolding opposite the present Hastings Avenue
Photograph courtesy of the Imperial War Museum, London. H 11548.

*To defend against an attack from the wide open spaces behind Brooklands
at Jaywick, this pillbox was constructed at the end of Rover Avenue.
It still remains to this day.*
Photograph courtesy of Fred Nash, ECC

Despite the graffiti, which causes no structural harm, the pillbox at Grasslands, Jaywick, survives in reasonable condition with its Turnbull machine-gun mounting (Bottom) still intact.

Photograph courtesy of Fred Nash, ECC

From its boundary with Frinton-on-Sea at Sandy Point, where Holland Marshes meet the sea shore, there was a series of concrete pillboxes built along the sea wall. Where the sea wall ends and the cliff gradually rises there were further pillboxes. Close to the sluice exit, the ground rises more significantly into a cliff which continues all the way to West Clacton. At The Gap, near the present Clacton Sailing Club premises, where there was an access point from the sea, anti-invasion scaffolding angled on two sides was erected. On the cliff top at the junction of Haven Avenue with The Esplanade, there was a pillbox and a spigot mortar position. Nearby on the top of the cliff there was a pillbox disguised within a wooden shelter. Rolled lengths of barbed wire lined the cliff top either side of The Esplanade. Below Southview Drive, on a short length of privately constructed sea wall, there was another pillbox and wiring. There were further pillboxes on the cliff top at the ends of York Road, Kings Avenue and Sea Lane.

Prior to 1938, the cliffs and foreshore had been in private ownership. Various substantial wooden bathing, amusement and refreshment pavilions had been built at the foot of the cliffs. One of these, a refreshment pavilion below the junction of York Road and The Kings Parade, was requisitioned. The interior was stripped out, and a concrete pillbox constructed on the wood floor. A testament to the strength of the original construction! A further pavilion, used for amusements, and of a similar size, was located on the beach approximately between Kings Avenue and the Hazlemere Road car park. This also had a pillbox constructed within. These pavilions made a perfect disguised defence position.

A major defence installation on the cliff top opposite Hazlemere and Lyndhurst Roads was the Coastal Defence Battery. It comprised two concrete emplacements, each containing an ex-naval six inch gun. Camouflage netting covered the installation. On each side of these emplacements there was a coastal artillery searchlight, partly set into the cliff top. Nearby were all the associated buildings necessary to support these guns. Towards the Kingscliff Hotel there was a concrete tower which was the battery observation post, with its attendant pillbox. The whole area had extensive barbed wiring, weapons pits, trenches and excavations. This Coastal Defence Battery was constructed during 1940, and records show that in October the site was manned by 331 Battery.

Airborne invasion

The landscape at Holland-on-Sea towards the north included the Great Holland marshes. A large flat open area beyond the built up area of the village was a potential landing ground for an airborne invasion attack. A range of defences were put in place as a counter measure. At Holland Haven near the sluice gates was a pillbox, prominent on an eminence which narrows towards the seashore, and still in existence to this day. The entrance to this pillbox is at the seaward side, indicating that its purpose was to defend from an inland attack. South westwards, and off Manor Road, there was another pillbox, again overlooking the marshes and the B1032 road to Great Holland.

From Bolters Dump, once located alongside Frinton Road, opposite the junction with Brighton Road, there was a clear view across to the marshes. Here a concentration of defence works were built. These included two pillboxes, a concrete weapons pit, and two other weapon pits. There was also wiring, including a dividing stretch of wiring across the site. Equally important, there were two field lavatories for use by the soldiers!

Between Brentwood and Slade roads there was a major gunsite, located close to Ipswich Road. Here were substantial concrete installations for two Howitzer type guns, with one positioned in front of the other on this gently sloping site. An ancillary brick building, and other smaller structures were all part of this site which had considerable wiring entanglements surrounding it.

A description and location of the anti-invasion defences at Jaywick.

Jaywick, to the south-west of Clacton-on-Sea offered a different range of anti-invasion defence works. The prime defence was a series of pillboxes along the seawall, and construction works were underway from late 1940. A pillbox at the Martello Tower at Brooklands continued a line of such defences from St. Osyth. It was followed by more pillboxes, probably every 200/300 yards along the coast to Clacton Golf Course. Aerial photographs from the 1940's show the distinctive hexagonal shape on the seawall at Lion Point, Beach Way, opposite Cornflower Road and at the east end of The Close. Two more were on the beach at the golf course. However, it is virtually certain that there would have been more than this, probably at least a dozen in total to maintain an uninterrupted web of crossfire.

Dannert wiring and slit trenches complemented the pillboxes. On the beach stretched a line of scaffolding, similar to that previously described at Clacton-on-Sea.

As a back-up to these primary defences, there were secondary defences. At Beach Way, in the Arcadia Car Park, opposite The Morocco, wiring was stretched along the seawall and across the roadway. Nearby at number 39, the veranda entrance was requisitioned and provided with sandbagging for a defence point. Also in this road at four separate plots, fences were removed and weapon pits made. Just south west, at the end of Meadow Way, Grants Stores, was requisitioned and the shop made into a strong point with the flat roof of the premises provided with sandbagging to protect a Light Machine Gun. At number 1 Broome Way, westwards of Beach Way, provision was made for a gun emplacement. Also in this road at four consecutive plots fences were taken down and weapon pits constructed. Lion Point, with its attendant pillboxes was obviously seen as a key position to defend.

Another flat roof, this time at number 8 Sea Flowers Way, was the site of a machine gun post which was protected by sandbagging. Three roads along, at Sea Cornflower Way, numbers 5 and 7, there were rifle posts with wiring and sandbagging.

Anti-tank obstacles in the form of large concrete cubes were positioned in a line east and west of the golf course. The ground hereabouts consists of marshy areas, and to provide a physical barrier steel hawsers were in places stretched between the concrete cubes.

The wide open spaces inland and to the north, of the Grasslands area, was a potential site for an airborne landing. A dyke with a embankment here was a defence in itself but it was also the site of two pillboxes. One, still surviving, was at the end of Rover Avenue, the other was north of Sea Way situated at a bend in the dyke's course. This pillbox also survives to this day. Beyond the dyke the land gently rises up towards Cockett Wick Farm. East of this farm house site, partially hidden in a ditch, were a line of five

Astonishingly, at least a small part of the steel hawser which stretched between the concrete cubes still survives beneath the rough ground near the golf course.

brick and concrete machine gun positions. Two further machine gun posts were on a field boundary at right angles to these. The field of fire from this gently elevated position across to Grasslands and Brooklands would have been considerable.

The Tudor area of the Jaywick Sands Estate was another defence site. At Crossways, on a building plot, was a sandbagged gun position, together with a partly built brick pillbox covered by a beach hut. At the south east corner of Tudor Green there were a number of weapon pits. The construction programme of all these defence works, and the adaption of buildings, was completed by December 1941.

The next stage of defence works began in early 1943 with a light anti-aircraft gun site being located on an empty building plot number 15 at Park Square West, Tudor Green. This site later developed into a heavy anti-aircraft gun site, with associated facilities necessary for its support.

3

Removing the defences

The removal of the war time defences, and getting back to the holiday business

From 1943 the course of the war was steadily turning in favour of the Allies, but the military influence and controls were to last well beyond the eventual end of hostilities in 1945 in Clacton and the surrounding district.

The strict ban on visitors who had no special reason to visit the coastal areas from The Wash to Lymington in Hampshire, was partially lifted by the War Office on 25th August 1944[3], although there had been some relaxation in the previous three summers. The War Office reminded the public that these areas were still regulated, with some beaches closed because of the minefields, and that telescopes or binoculars were not to be used. At this same time the Clacton Urban District Council was beginning a programme of 'clearing up' the seafront, and discussing future improvement plans and the repair of enemy-damaged property. Some of the ornamental gardens on the seafront were opened for the first time since 1939[4]. A further sign that the threat of invasion was lessening was the decision in November 1944 to dissolve the Clacton Invasion Committee.

At Jaywick, as early as 1943 some defence positions were derequisitioned, notably those on the flat roofs of properties. The land where there were weapon pits was handed back to the owners between 1943 and 1945. The Grasslands area to the north of Brooklands was not released until December 1949, and it was to be June 1950 when the former Acadia car-park owners eventually received its notice of derequision.

Signs that the military requirements were being scaled down at Clacton-on-Sea were shown in January 1945 when the War Office stated that they no longer required the public conveniences opposite the Oulton Hall Hotel[5].

---

3   East Essex Gazette 26th August 1944.
4   EEG 16th September 1944.
5   ERO A6083, and subsequent references. CUDC correspondence files 1944-50.

Also in January, the War Department relinquished its interest at the Albany Gardens defence works and also at the Anglefield gardens. Within five weeks some sixty-two more properties were to be released by the military. The Urban District Council were pressing for more de-requisitions, and on the 29th January they sent a letter to the Ministry of Transport War, asking why the road blocks could not now be removed. A reply came from the Lands Branch of Eastern Command which informed them by letter on 17th February that:

'No portion of the sea front from Butlin's to the Coastguard Station at Holland Haven has yet been de-requisitioned. The area extends from the seaward side to low water mark up to the Parade at the Cliff top. Additionally no member of the public is allowed on the same, except council employees to carry out maintenance works.'

Within a few days the Council received an up-dated letter stating that:

'No part of the sea front is de-requisitioned yet, except that between Penfold Road and (the now demolished) Passmore Edwards Home at Connaught Gardens.'

Work commences

The type of defences which had been constructed had used concrete, steel and timber, utilised in various ways. The Clacton Urban District Council were informed by the War Office in January 1945, of a list of materials which they no longer had an interest in. This list included: angle irons and steel scrap, tubular scaffolding, and the steel and timber anti-aircraft deterrent poles. The removal, transportation and storage of these materials was to cause problems for the Council.

From March 1945, the Council sought tenders for the demolition and removal of concrete structures on Clacton sea-front in connection with the cliff, greenswards and the promenades, so that work could begin. On May 11th, the Council advertised by public notice that all the public and communal shelters in the Urban District would be closed from that date, three days after Victory in Europe day (VE day).

Some clearance of the defences began in early 1945. Workmen are clearing barbed wire here at Holland-on-Sea

The concrete pimples located at the road junctions adjoining the Marine Parade were being removed from July. The 16th Holding Batallion, and the Garrison Engineer supplied Italian Prisoners of War (POW) for the work. Work began from Connaught Gardens and progressed towards Edith Road. On the 16th July work was recorded as taking place at Tower Road, with just two more roads still to be cleared.

The next task for the POW labour, was the removal of the reinforced concrete pillbox and the associated concrete tank blocks at the junction of Holland Road with Sladburys Lane. Another group were busy at a similar site in Cloes Lane. The reinforcing bars within the concrete made the work difficult and slow.

The local Council helped the military and the POW labour by hiring out the compressor and concrete breaker from their Gas and Water Departments. The broken up lumps of concrete then had to be transported to the Council's depot at Northbourne Road. There was just one 30cwt. lorry available for the work, and this was only occasionally available! The Council responded during July 1945 by themselves hiring both labour and transport from Messrs Fairclough Brothers of Clacton, at a rate of 4/- (20p) per ton. In a report to council members on 16th July 1945, it was recorded that to date nearly 100 tons of concrete had been removed from where the defences had been broken up, to the council yard. There remained a further 140 tons of still stacked up on the footways of the respective roads.

The beach at Holland-on-Sea at the end of the war.
In addition to all the anti-invasion defences, cliff slips had caused
movement to the sea walls and beach huts

The Pier Gap had been a well defended place. The machine gun points and the Alan Williams turrets here were removed, and the road reinstated. Mr Aiston, the town surveyor, informed the council that work was also now underway to remove the defences at North Road and Thorpe Road. On completion of this work it was reported that all the former defence works the Council were responsible for had now been removed.

The defences removal programme was not without its problems. The Kings Parade at Holland-on-Sea, had some iron obstructions which had been left protruding above ground level, and a visitor tripped over an obstruction causing herself an injury to her knee and wrist.

The scale of the procedures necessary between the War Office and the local authority also involved the disconnection of water and electricity services, with all its payments and necessary associated paperwork; then the reconnection of the services for the de-requisitioned property for the owners and occupiers returning to the town after evacuation. In some cases considerable damage had been done to property by the troops billeted in them, and claims were made for which an agreement of compensation had to be settled.

In May 1945 the absent owner of Apsley House in Penfold Road wished to regain occupancy once again to his property. However, Lt. Colonel B. Hinkley QC at Colchester, informed him that:

'Apsley House is in a block of accommodation reserved for the ATS[6], and is in full occupation, and it is not likely to be released until the whole block in Penfold Road is vacated, and there is no sign of this happening at present.'

The owner of a property named 'Inworth' in Wash Lane had his home used by the military as a Dental Centre. The owner of the 'Lonsdale Cafe' on the Marine Parade was informed early in 1945 that it had been derequisitioned, but this was soon followed by a further communication stating that the notice had been cancelled. There were many similar such problems for the owners of requisitioned properties.

The town was desperate to get back to its original purpose of providing holiday facilities for visitors. The East Coast resorts, including Clacton-on-Sea, became aware that the war time defences on the South Coast resorts were being cleared first, to the detriment of those in the East. Mr C. B. Hearn for Clacton Council, stated that less than half the beach would be open for the approaching Easter holiday, mainly due to the danger of mines. Mr Hearn had been informed by the War Office that they could not spare any more trained mine detectors. Holland-on-Sea and Jaywick beaches would still be closed over the 1945 Easter period with a consequent loss of revenue. This was not the case with the South Coast resorts[7].

---

6 Auxiliary Territorial Service
7 Egyptian Gazette 25th March 1945.

Following a protest by the Council, the War Department's Land Agent agreed to visit the local resorts on the 23rd April 1945[8], to discuss any difficulties that might exist, and which the military might be able to assist with, as to the use of beaches for holiday purposes. No doubt some searching questions were put to the Land Agent!

The problems with the minefield clearance

The work to clear the various minefields seems to have begun in March 1945, although checks were made from 1943 of the actual numbers of mines currently existing, compared to those originally laid. The actual clearance programme was to be a long process with many complications and anxieties for the military authorities, residents and council officials alike.

Minefield 45/40 was on the Holland Marshes. The number of mines laid here was recorded as being 207. There were 194 mines cleared, with 21 'old craters' found. On the 13th September 1945, the military issued a clearance certificate signed by T. E. Chad, Brigadier, Commander, NE Essex Sub-District, to the CUDC, stating that the area had been swept more than once using the PMD[9] method, and was considered safe. The perimeter fences and noticeboards had already been removed.

Minefield 45/41 and 45/41a at Holland-on-Sea cliffs, partly on the cliff face and extending to the clifftop, were swept several times by the military using the PMD system, but they refrained from issuing a clearance certificate. The next year, in March 1946, the Military reported that there were no mines on field 45/41, but at minefield 45/41a, the perimeter fence was repaired and further warning notices erected as a precaution for the public.

At the end of May 1946, the CUDC were concerned about this minefield at Holland-on-Sea, and the apparent lack of activity by the military authorities. The summer visitors were expected, and they and the residents could not currently use the clifftop area. Eventually, on the 1st July 1946, the mine clearance certificates were issued for both these minefields by the military. Unfortunately, the CUDC never received the certificates, and the saga dragged on until December 1946 when it was satisfactorily concluded

---

8 The Agent visited Harwich, Frinton & Walton, Brightlingsea, and then Clacton at 1600 hours.
9 Polish Mine Detector

following the successful intervention of the local MP, Sir Stanley Holmes.

The reason for the long delay in the mine clearance was that part of the area within the wired enclosure of 45/41a, was believed to be a dummy field, but was treated as a 'live minefield.' The nearby minefield 45/41 also caused problems despite being swept firstly during the summer of 1943, by a field company of the Czech Independent Brigade, then again early the next year by the Royal Engineers, but in February 1944, two mines were found washed up on the beach at the foot of this minefield. This minefield had been laid in December 1940 by 279 Field Company, Royal Engineers. They never realised the problems their work would later cause.

The next minefield, 45/42 at Eastcliff, had 216 mines laid in four parallel rows. During late 1942, the military exploded 113 mines in the two inland rows, and then re-aligned the fence. In January 1944 the minefield was re-swept, and then again during October 1945. A clearance certificate was finally issued on the 5th January 1946, after the two attempts at a clearance. The local residents were concerned that the perimeter fences still remained in place when the summer was coming to an end. The CUDC were

COAST ROAD, HOLLAND-ON-SEA. 63231.

A post-war view showing where minefield 54/42 had been located on the Greensward, and which had caused clearance problems

informed that there was a shortage of military personnel to carry out the removal work. After the long years of war, 'normality' was slow to return for the townspeople.

The group of four minefields, 45/43, 44, 45, and 46 on Clacton Golf Course, contained a total of 812 mines. Although there were discrepancies recorded during clearance works with the total numbers originally laid, the number of mines cleared, and 'old craters' found, the War Department Lands Branch reported to the Urban District Council, that these minefields had been declared safe. They had been re-swept after soil disturbance had been caused as a result of breaches in the sea wall. At the conclusion of the work, the military could give *'No guarantee'* that the area was safe!

Information about the Jaywick minefield clearance works does not appear to have survived.

The clearance continues

The scope of the military presence in the Clacton-on-Sea area was widespread and varied. During January 1945, the Albany Gardens trenching and sandbagging defence works were declared redundant, and

The West Greensward at Clacton-on-Sea about 1946, surrounded by fencing to protect the newly sown grass. The lighting standards along the cliff top have still yet to be reinstated

The former six-inch coastal artillery gun site opposite Hazlemere Road in 1947.
The lower picture shows demolition work underway.

This pillbox near The Haven, at Holland-on-Sea as it was in 1957,
was to remain into the 1970's when the crumbling sea wall was
replaced with new sea defences.

the triangular pre-war gardens at Anglefield, which had an assortment of military hutments, was also relinquished by the War Department. Military use however extended well beyond, in certain places, V.E. Day in May 1945. The Street Fighting Area[10] in the town was not cancelled until 4th September 1945. The Council was informed that from 9th November 1945 the Training Area in Old Road would no longer be required. Another Military Training Area located at Lancaster Gardens was not released until June 1946.

Some Clactonians were directly affected by the remaining defences. One being a local fisherman, Mr Tucker during June 1945. The two concrete ramped slopes to the beach either side of the pier entrance had anti-invasion blocks across them. Those on the West Beach side had been removed, but those on the East side remained. Restrictions on the use of rowing boats had recently been withdrawn, but Mr Tucker could only launch his boat on the West Beach, then make the long row around the end of the pier to reach his fishing grounds off the East Beach. His wish for their removal was eventually granted.

Clacton's famous gardens all required re-planting. These new flower beds close to the Band Pavilion were among those being re-established after the war.

10 Records do not exist to describe this area.

Reinstatement works underway on the East Promenade at Clacton which is covered with construction equipment. A derrick is located at the pier entrance.

The long years of war had a devastating effect on the seafront promenades and greenswards, and they had quickly become overgrown. When the cliff-top was relinquished by the Military Authorities early in 1945, the CUDC was anxious to allow public access once again. Such was its state, the Council was forced to prevent the public using a major portion of its length. Early in the summer, the council gardeners were able to clear a short section east of the Band Pavilion; then, the 16th Holding Battalion provided Military labour to supplement the council gardeners to clear the whole of the eastern promenade up to just beyond Connaught Gardens. During August, work then was able to commence westwards of the pier. Upon clearance, the greenswards were re-seeded and then surrounded with chestnut paling fencing for protection. In the following summer season of 1946 the council's garden superintendent Mr J Douglas reported that the fencing should remain as the grass was not yet established. Reinstatement of the seafront to pre-war standards was frustratingly slow!

The CUDC were seeking tenders into the New Year of 1947, during a severe winter of snow falls and low temperatures, to further continue defence clearance works. Reed & Mallik of Station Road, Clacton, and C Foster Hughes of High Street, Walton-on-the-Naze, both applied to clear the defences from Holland Haven to Passmore Edwards Home, near Connaught Gardens. The work involved removing and disposing of the barbed wire, and its supporting iron stakes. Additionally, to remove and dispose of the anti-invasion scaffolding on the beach. Foster Hughes provided the lowest tender at £666 which was accepted by the council. During the clearance of these defences, it was reported at a Holland-on-Sea Ratepayers Meeting that the removed barbed wire was piled up like haystacks along the cliff top, making it an eyesore for residents and visitors alike[11].

Clacton Pier was breached in two places during the war, once by an enemy mine, then by the military as an anti-invasion measure. The wide concrete section shown is where the Crystal Casino stood pre-war. Towards the right-hand side of the pier head, the former Bertram's Children's Theatre has recently been demolished. Contractors equipment is still in evidence.
Photograph by D. Constance

The Lilley Farm Beach, a pre-war private beach with beach huts and other facilities, owned by Mrs Felkin, was not handed back by the Military until

---

11 EEG February 14th 1946.

the 25th April 1947. Located at Eastcliff, there had been much military activity here. At the same time the nearby former six-inch Coastal Defence Battery was also being demolished, the breeches to the guns having been removed previously.

The Holland-on-Sea beach had also been in private ownership pre-war. It had been divided into sections. One lessee, Walter Johnson, had invested heavily from 1929 by building a series of substantial wooden beach pavilions. These were painted in alternate orange and white horizontal stripes. The War Department had requisitioned all five pavilions on this section of beach in June 1940. All five were surrounded by Dannert wiring. Two pavilions had concrete pillboxes constructed within, giving the perfect camouflaged positions. Cliff falls and storms caused movement to the pavilions, and when eventually in May 1947 they were de-requisitioned, only one was to be reinstated. The remainder were taken down as being deemed beyond repair.

A further two years were to elapse before the military were to release approximately three acres of the Greensward on the Marine Parade. Unfortunately the records do not indicate where this site was, but it was likely to be at Eastcliff where the minefield was once located. The Council began the reinstatement of the greenswards, and enclosed them with chestnut paling fencing. Mr J Douglas the CUDC Gardens Superintendent, requested that the fencing be retained for a second year to prevent any damage to the grass by the public.

By January 1948 all the war time damage to the pier had been repaired, and during the summer season the swimming pool was in use once again. The P. S. "Golden Eagle" resumed its pleasure trips from the pier berthing arm after a nine year lapse. From the West Beach, the "Viking Saga" pleasure boat operated again. The next year, in 1949, the newly built "Queen of the Channel"[12] made her first day trip to France from Clacton, carrying 1,472 passengers. The Clacton Golf Course which had closed in June 1940 reopened on the 1st November. For the summer season of 1950, the Ramblas Concert Party, which had been a pre-war favourite on the pier, restarted their open air concerts. The town was in business once again.

---

12 This vessel replaced the first 'Queen of the Channel' which was lost at Dunkirk in 1940.

As the new decade of 1950 approached the reinstatement of the central part of the seafront at Clacton was at last completed. However many former defences still remained, especially the pillboxes. These were either on private land or at low priority sites at Holland-on-Sea and at Jaywick.

Clacton-on-Sea, Holland-on-Sea and Jaywick were once again busy providing exciting holiday destinations for the citizens living in post-war austerity Britain.

What remains today?

It must be said that such was the desire, immediately after the war, to clear the beaches and seafront of the concrete and steel defence works that not a great deal survived the post-war years. With the return of the holidaymakers firmly in mind, work began straight away, and now, sixty-odd years later, a guiding hand may be required to track down some of the less obvious remains.

Nothing survives of the anti-invasion scaffolding which stretched for so far along the beach and, immediately behind it on the promenade and along the cliff face, every one of the hundreds of concrete anti-tank blocks has gone, but, almost of curosity value now, the remains of these blocks can still be seen in one place. Behind the beach huts on the promenade opposite Collingwood Road a short retaining wall has been built out of the broken-up anti-invasion blocks! Rather than cart them away from the promenade it was clearly a lot more convenient to use some of the pieces virtually on site. As confirmation of their origin, many of the pieces can be seen with the indentations made by the steel re-inforcement bars. Others show flat faces with the marks left by the wooden shuttering when they were first cast on the promenade.

Of the pillboxes there is mixed survival. In Clacton-on-Sea and along the frontage of built-up Holland-on-Sea, Clacton-on-Sea nothing survives to show where they once stood. However, east of The Gap at Holland Haven and along the seawall towards Frinton there are some fine examples. The Holland Haven pillbox has undergone a number of phases of evolution. It was first built as a basic hexagonal pillbox guarding the flat lands behind the seawall against paratroop attack. Shortly afterwards, perhaps only weeks later, a concrete "skirt" was added to give further protection. In

This pillbox at Holland Haven Country Park is one of those still remaining today. It is easily accessible to view.

modern times, it was adapted as a viewing platform for Holland Haven Country Park with steps, a handrail and notice board added, although this has now gone.

Further along the seawall, at Chevaux de Frise Point, there is the fascinating sight of, seemingly, a pillbox with no loopholes! In fact, it is the surviving base with a staircase inside which led up to the pillbox which stood on the top. The pillbox was taken down, leaving the access base. Within a hundred yards there is an example of what it once looked like, a rare complete pillbox of this unusual design. Crossing the Holland-on-Sea parish boundary at Sandy Point there is another of the same pattern.

At Jaywick, two more pillboxes still survive. Those along the seafront have long gone but two of those which guarded the "back door" are still there, still overlooking the flat lands to the north.

It is difficult to imagine that all trace of the huge six-inch gun battery, with its casemates, ammunition stores, look-out towers and searchlight emplacements can have gone. But such is the case. It is now an open

The Pier Gap, and Pier Avenue area was heavily defended during the war.
This post-war photograph shows no evidence remaining of the former defences.

greensward, as it was in the 1930's.

The many road barriers which sealed off Clacton-on-Sea were of two types. The permanent ones, with anti-tank pimples concreted into the surface right across the pavement and the roadway in between, and the removable ones which had pimples on the pavements but lengths of steel standing in sockets across the roadway. Although each and every one of the hundreds of pimples has gone, the signs of their previous existence can still be made out in a couple of places. When each pimple and its concrete footing was lifted out of the road surface it left a large hole, which was filled in and tarmac'd over. Over sixty years later, the filling and the tarmac is starting to sink, or in some cases to rise. Across Lancaster Gardens West, Lancaster Gardens East, Albany Gardens West and Albany Gardens East the pattern of the rows of anti-tank pimples can be seen as circles in the tarmac about 2' 6" across. A bizarre and somewhat unexpected sight. Fortunately, hopefully, nothing of the minefields now survives!

Civil Defence played an immensely important role during World War Two. In 1938, in anticipation of the coming conflict, Clacton Urban District

Council set up a department to be responsible for the protection of the civilian population against the bombing raids which were sure to come. In a recruitment drive as many as 385 people volunteered to join the new service, the Air Raid Precautions unit, or A.R.P., an organisation which would be a mainstay of local defence during the testing time ahead. Clacton Urban District Council authorised ten A.R.P. Warden's posts to be built - at a cost of £49/7/6d each, plus 35/- for a window! Fortunately, a finely-surving example still stands at Holland-on-Sea, on the corner of Queensway and Dulwich Road. This was the command post for A.R.P. Sector B12.

Nearly seventy years after their construction, each of the surviving defences, has a part to play in telling the story of seaside Clacton, a front-line town during World War Two.